THE cottage BOOK

THE cottage BOOK

living simple and easy

CAROL BASS

photographs by Dennis Welsh

STEWART, TABORI & CHANG
NEW YORK

Contents

Foreword

I remember sitting on a cottage porch many summers ago. After swimming in the ocean all day, my mother brushed my wet hair into a tidy, neat ponytail, her deliberate brushstrokes seeming to move in time with the waves. The furniture on the wide porch consisted of two rockers, a white porch swing, and a card table where we often played double solitaire. Life in this little cottage made a big impression on me even as a child, and throughout the years some of my happiest moments have revolved around cottage life. It's my favorite way of living—pure and sweet like good local honey. There is a clarity and freedom in the air that allows wonderful pleasures to happen spontaneously, the kind of pleasures that are woven into rich and colorful occasions that bind families and friends together.

Cottage life entails a complete and utter lack of pretension. The simple houses we chose for this book are found in a wide range of landscapes—seaside, countryside, woodland—but they all have several things in common: simplicity, comfort, a close connection to nature, a recognition of the past, an occasionally daring use of color, and a wisp of humor. These deeply personal spaces reflect their owners' lives. Like the best cottages, they are uncomplicated, even humble, and unconcerned with high style and inflated tastes. And I chose them on the simplest of grounds. A subtle detail, usually having to do with color, would catch my eye for a moment—the red door of one cottage, a yellow table on the porch of another, twin pink bedspreads in another, a dark green screen door, aqua trim, white shutters. These cottages all have a story worth telling. I hope you enjoy this visual gift, a celebration, really, of the joys of cottage life.

Carol Bass

PART I
The Cottage Spirit

Nestled in fir trees, up a winding path from the granite shore and the cold, deep water, there's a lovely little house on an island in Maine that I think of as a perfect cottage. Owned by the same family for almost a century, it embodies all the ideals of a cottage and cottage life. A wonderful spirit shines in this cottage, one that is highly contagious.

A reverence for nature abides here. Bushy sweet fern and juniper grow luxuriantly all around, forming a lush, three-foot-high, ground-cover quilt. Paths crisscross this miniature jungle and lead to other cottages, connecting neighbors who share a love for the island.

This simple setting offers space, fresh air, and an unencumbered lifestyle that rejuvenates the soul. Old climbing roses on the fence out front, planted when the cottage was first built, amplify the feelings of welcome with their inviting color and scent. White rockers, heavy with layers of paint, are lined up on the porch, close enough to the railing so one can comfortably set down a cup of tea. Yet they offer just the right amount of space to stretch out and reflect as the sun goes down. The deep, mossy green of the porch, screen doors, and floorboards, as well as the weathered gray of the shingles, reflects the majesty and solitude of the surrounding rocks, woods, and water. Inside, dappled sun warms the big, bright kitchen, the social center of life in the house.

Each cottage has its own peculiar aroma, and inside this one's sun-yellow kitchen, familiar smells welcome and embrace family and visitors. Every cottage has a natural charisma, too, which is to say that it reflects the owner's way of living. "Cottage style" is not a particular look or something that can be created by hiring a decorator. An honesty is present in cottage living because simplicity, comfort, and ease are the priorities. Equally important is a respect for nature, for cottage culture lies deep in the outdoors. The desire to reconnect with the natural world and its healing ways is everpresent. Cottages are humble, tidy, sometimes even humorous examples of a spirited way of life, invigorating spaces where we meet ourselves again and reunite with the carefree ways of our childhood.

This book celebrates the cottage sensibility, one that whispers . . . *Stop. Step back. Remember what's important.* Cottage life is not about status, possessions, or glamour; it is about history, nature, simplicity, family and friends—things that really matter.

Buttery yellow walls and chairs and moss-painted floors are classic cottage touches.

The cottage has sported lively yellow shingles with turquoise shutters since at least 1942, when the owner's family purchased the cottage.

Vintage wicker, beadboard, expansive windows, summer gardens—the basic ingredients of cottage life.

That's why this book does not describe steps for creating a "cottage" look but instead offers many examples of how dwellers have created living spaces filled with uncomplicated furniture and objects. It is this approach that reflects the immediacy and vitality of cottage life—the opposite of artificiality.

Gathered on the following pages are a few of my favorite cottages. Part II, "Old Favorites," contains a wonderful group of original cottages built in the late nineteenth and early twentieth centuries—some virtually untouched by time, others transported quietly into the present through subtle and charming makeovers. Part III, "Fresh Ideas," looks at cottages where new ideas have been applied to classic structures—all the while respecting the cottage aesthetic.

But before we explore these individual cottages in detail, we need to examine what a cottage is by analyzing those elements that define it: the character of cottage architecture, the interior details, and the essence of cottage living.

Farmhouse sinks and open pantry shelving are remarkable examples of vintage cottage style. At left, the elegant kerosene lamp, wall-mounted with swinging arm brackets, tells a story of technological change over the life span of the cottage.

The Joy of Simplicity

Cottages have always been built for easy living, refuges from the hustle-bustle, places where life is meant to be as untroubled as possible. Informality is part of this lifestyle, as is a tendency to pare down rather than build up. Cottage life is a philosophy based on learning to relax and just be. An escape from the rhythms and burdens of daily life, cottage life embraces the freedom to walk down a one-lane road—leaving behind SUVs, televisions, neckties, and lipstick—and live the way we did as children, with spontaneity and energy. It is simplicity that reawakens this sense of wonderment and possibility.

Joy is never found in things; it's harbored deep inside us. Retreating to an open-air porch, sitting close to family and friends, is a direct route to the core of ourselves—an investment, surely, in our own survival.

Brightly painted furniture brings energy and spirit to a room sheathed in beadboard stained gray. The open shelving, typical in cottage construction, allows for handy access to the many quirky items a house like this collects over its lifetime.

A porch at sunset offers the essence of summer.

This suite of green wicker porch furniture with its gracefully rolled edges gives the porch an elegant turn-of-the century feeling.

A hammock is appropriate for a porch of the nineteenth *or* twenty-first century.

Mounds of scarlet baby zinnias attract late-summer butterflies.

A Connection to Nature

Living within the shelter of a cottage resting deeply in nature renews and sustains us. Memories of a child-hood spent close to the outdoors rise to the surface—staying up late when fireflies first appear, building fairy houses in the woods, feasting on wild blackberries, letting the rain on the roof send you safely to sleep.

In a cottage, one reconnects with the rhythms of nature. Whether lakeside, on the ocean shore, in the deep woods, or on rolling farmland, a cottage life celebrates the five senses and heightens our awareness of them. The smell of sea air is invigorating and the sand underneath our feet is cool and soothing. Walks in the quiet woods calm us, for the scent is deeply familiar there, a mingling of pine, moss, and fern. Picking bouquets of wildflowers for the kitchen table, we understand the summer landscape as a predictable sequence, beginning with golden buttercups and ending with autumn's purple asters. The day's activities are tailored to the natural world and what it provides.

Living in a natural environment, we reacquaint ourselves with real time. At the cottage, time is not meas-ured by goals or achievements, but by nature's cycles.

This is why gardening is so much a part of cottage life. Cottage gardens have an effusive and casual quality that rejuvenates us. Tending the summer flowers gives us time for quiet meditation among beautiful colors and forms, be they blooming lilies or the birds and butterflies that visit the garden all summer long.

Nested among autumn birches, a small cottage awaits its owners.

With simple majesty, the three-story, pyramid-topped tower of this cottage and a stately conifer stand sentinel over the azure water and rocky coast. One can only admire the balance the builder-architect struck between the site and the structure: In the face of the dramatic trio of rock, water, and sky, he chose to utilize handsome clean lines and symmetry, adding a little flair with the tower and roof lines. The carefully adorned cottage is a little like a well-bred Yankee lady dressed up for a dance—it has just enough makeup, but not too much. The two-board shutters offer a touch of finesse, but in subdued, weathered tones.

Many cottage lovers covet the patina of the worn, painted board wall behind the drop-leaf farm table. Nail holes, thumb tacks, and a bit of wear only add to the charming effect. Tins of all shapes and sizes and glass jars are ubiquitous in cottage pantries to keep staples crisp. The fluted and ruffled serving and compote bowls—works of art, their crazed surfaces offering evidence of decades of use—presently hold garlic and onions.

The crisp spread and simple furnishings in afternoon light give this room a feeling of quiet repose, but the quirky heart-backed chair adds a little whimsy. The sloped walls of the room create a cocooning effect.

A Reverence for History

The past comes alive in old cottages. Beloved traditions are celebrated and honored: Eating chowder on the porch, picking wild berries for muffins, reading in the cool, sweet-smelling barn.

Here, history provides the framework for contemporary life, so little has been modernized. Cherished antique furniture and dishes are used daily, old lamps cast a familiar glow, electrical wiring is in view, and pencil marks on the wall, a record of children growing taller, remain for generations.

Even in newer cottages, quality vintage pieces with desired associations to the past—wicker, pottery, and textiles, painted doors and salvaged wood, windows mellowed by the years—create a reassuring sense of the continuum of cottage life and impart grace and character.

Elements of Cottage Style

If simplicity, nature, and history are the intangibles that inform the cottage ideal, the design elements in both old and modern cottages are the concrete tools residents employ as they shape their dream.

On the exterior, clapboard as well as painted shingles, shutters, and trim dress up and personalize a cottage. Natural cedar shingles, gracefully aged by time and weather, are the basis for another classic cottage look.

Porches and fireplaces are the central social areas, drawing people like bees to honey. The porch is the outer world, a fresh-air parlor where painted and woven rockers, vintage wicker, and lazy hammocks offer the pleasures of quiet rest. The fireplace is the heart of the more private, inner world, the soul of the house and a sacred space where loved ones join in the intimate rite of sharing reflections and telling the day's news. Stones and shells, even timbers found on beaches and in nearby fields, are evocative materials for the construction of the hearth.

Fluid social spaces for large family gatherings or small groups of friends are inviting, with soft sofas and comfortable chairs pulled close to the hearth. Areas for socializing tend to be cozy and informal. These

There is no shortage of comfortable seating in this cottage parlor.

The drama of the driftwood bench and its shadows is only partially subdued by the magnificent scenery behind it. The bench—a whimsical seaside take on the rustic garden seat, which is more often composed of branches such as oak—accompanies a rocking chair with an unusual herringbone-woven seat and back.

This kitchen was expanded in recent years and brought up to date without losing the classic cottage touches.

are uncluttered spaces, with bright color and art, books, family photographs, and games, lending the cottage personality and individuality.

The textures of beadboard and bare wood bring a fresh, outdoorsy vitality to a cottage interior. In earlier times, the open-frame method of construction was the easiest, quickest, and most direct way of building a getaway in the woods. Today, that process and ambience is still desirable and emulated in new cottage construction. In houses built in the open-frame style, one is close to nature. The wood is warm and inviting, even sensual.

Often bare wood is painted to enliven a space. Green-painted floors have a grassy summer feel; old porch ceilings, painted sky blue, enhance the airy quality. Creamy-white-painted boards soften the atmosphere, providing additional surfaces where light can reflect.

Once furniture arrives in a cottage, it tends to stay, even when a dwelling changes hands, which may explain why so much furniture in cottages is often painted. Some pieces make their way to a cottage as

A hanging pendant light over the billiards table exhibits exposed electrical wiring. In some cottages, ceiling and wall construction was commonly left open to show studs and beams; when electricity came long after the initial construction, the wiring was left exposed.

Classic and pristine, a group of white Adirondack chairs are clustered in a backyard garden.

Vintage wicker chairs are brought to new life with pine green and calypso red paint.

castoffs from a year-round residence; a colorful coat of paint can handily integrate a dark, "serious" piece of furniture into a more casual setting. Paint also stands up well to rough weather and sweaty glasses of lemonade.

Primitive pieces like twig furniture and claw-foot tubs are treasured for their direct, easygoing style, too, and they give a sense of history to newer cottages. Likewise, vintage wicker and rattan pieces, as well as Adirondack chairs—old cottage classics—are dependable standbys for outdoor seating. Freshening up old wicker pieces with lively color can add great zest and heartiness to a room. Newer, unfussy pieces are wonderful when integrated with older furniture.

A small wonder of taking possession of a cottage is the treasure trove of china, silver, and serving pieces that, like the furniture, often remain with the structure. The pieces seem to tell a story: When a cottage remains in a family over many years, the old plates and bowls speak of all that is good and true about generations of cottage living and dining.

Cottage bedrooms tend to be simple and functional, too. These are unadorned and contemplative spaces, private hideaways meant for rest and solitude.

Cottages today provide us with a sense of constancy that is elusive in our often-chaotic lives. It is my hope that in this book you will find that no matter what form a family takes, no matter how far we roam, we always come home to the cottage.

Porch corners hold opportunities for sneaking away for a peaceful afternoon nap.

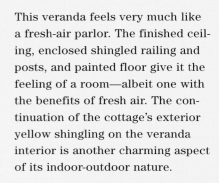

This veranda feels very much like a fresh-air parlor. The finished ceiling, enclosed shingled railing and posts, and painted floor give it the feeling of a room—albeit one with the benefits of fresh air. The continuation of the cottage's exterior yellow shingling on the veranda interior is another charming aspect of its indoor-outdoor nature.

The open-framed walls of this house are reminiscent of the more rustic style of some early cottages. With the fireplace wall sporting vertical boards and the adjacent wall, horizontal ones, the mood is casual; a creamy coat of paint is a bright touch. An opening off the living room reveals a cheerful, sunny dining room with green-painted floors, vintage painted chairs, and a dark wood table.

PART II
Old Favorites

The old cottages featured in this section are venerable jewels, plein-air havens where the pleasures of outdoor life have been enjoyed for well over a century. Most were built during the post–Civil War years, and the latter decades of the Victorian era (1880–1901), when notions of a simpler life grew in appeal, in part through the writing of Ralph Waldo Emerson and Henry David Thoreau. Fleeing the heavy, brocade-curtained windows of city dwellings for fresh country air, people originally lodged in tents, then rented rooms in guest houses and rambling inns, and finally purchased plots of land where they built their own personal retreats. The cottages included here were not constructed by wealthy industrialists but by humbler folk—teachers and ministers, for example, who continued America's pioneering attitude and lust for adventure out in the wild.

Lovely traditions flourish at a cottage—family weddings in rolling pastures or by the shore, summer birthdays on the porch, picnics under a full moon. A family's journey through time is measured out phase by phase by these rituals. Through them, a cottage becomes a ceremonial gathering place.

Many cottages have remained in the same family for generations. The clan that owns the cottage Southwind has been fortunate and wise enough to acquire several neighboring cottages over the years, so that their stronghold resembles a kid's rambling summer camp. Family members come from around the globe to gather each summer. In this manner, a cottage has become the ideal for the dream of stability in a volatile world.

CHAPTER 1
THE red doors OF southwind

A shore cottage called Southwind is aptly named for the wind that races over the water every summer afternoon, promptly around one o'clock. The cottage itself is a big, gleaming white rectangular box with an attached porch, but its simple lines give it a friendly appeal. A giant oak stands by the corner of the porch, and a small private beach is within jumping distance of the front steps. When all the family is gathered here on a hot day, the water is teeming with small boats, inner tubes, and floats. The activity is so grand it resembles a lively public beach. The cottage is south-facing, and from the shore the geese have a clear shot to Florida.

Red geraniums mimic the blazing red-painted doors and porch chairs. That's the part that draws everyone in: those red doors. They are so personal, so inviting. At dusk, the yellow-orange light at the back door matches the light inside, a warm golden glow that welcomes passersby and members of the extended family visiting from nearby cottages. The red gingham curtains in the back window are reminiscent of a time when people used to iron and bake every day, and they also make one want to know the people inside.

Unadorned and crisp, Southwind is a place of pure spiritual harmony, a composition of reserved form, a quirky passion for a slice of color. Inside it's tidy, the owners enjoy each other's company and celebrate their connections with the past.

Built in the mid-1890s, this cottage seems timeless, but a little detective work uncovers a century's worth of change in the form of small alterations and technical improvements. The current owner notes with wry amusement that a good chunk of his summer vacation each year is spent under the cottage, jacking it up, as it was built on posts without a foundation. But an hour spent enjoying the porch puts all the work into perspective for him.

Today, the cottage has electricity and plumbing, but in the 1890s there were kerosene lamps rather than light bulbs, and chunks of ice kept food and drinks cold. The unfinished, open framing characteristic of summer-cottage interiors allows interested parties to see the electrical wiring as it appeared on the day it was installed.

Some three decades after this first cottage was restored, one of the family's sons, now a retired doctor and grandfather, purchased the little house across the street. Of its three previous owners, he knew two and one was a relative, so he was familiar with the cottage and lured by its porch and view.

With its lively red rocking chairs, the porch on the shore side is the social heart of the cottage. Three generations of the family gather for morning coffee on the porch when the water is serene and as smooth as glass. By one o'clock, the prevailing south wind for which the cottage is named kicks in a little and ruffles the water. The color of the rockers echoes the red decorative accents in the interior; they are perhaps the favorite chairs in the cottage.

The current family progressed from renters to multigenerational cottage owners in a story that is typical of the growth of summer colonies. Since the 1930s, five generations of this family have now summered on the island. They stayed in rented cottages until they took the next step— a big one, requiring vision and moxie. In the lean years after the Great Depression, they bought an abandoned summer cottage on the isolated island.

Summering on the island required leisure time during the warm months. Because the schedules of ministers and teachers permitted them to spend a couple of months away from home each year, many summer cottagers came from these professions. In this family, the father, a minister, and the mother, an organist, shifted their pastoral duties to others back home so they could spend the summer months on the island. However, never remote from their calling, they held summertime Sunday church services on the wharf; they stored the pump organ in the post office/store during the week.

The vintage boat model, which has a permanent berth above the door, leads one's eyes—and heart—toward the spectacular vista of the ocean just beyond the cottage. Seen through the wavy old glass of the original windows, the boats on the water seem to bob even when the waters are calm.

The pass-through from the kitchen to the living room has become a compact vertical office in this classic turn-of-the-century cottage. In the well-worn corridor one can find ferry schedules, tide tables, maps, charts, and a rolling paper pad for notes. A handbell sits at the ready for an important call—dinner.

The open shelving offers a ready study of the casual dining that is typical of cottage life. For this family, the sturdy chowder bowls and coffee mugs work as well on the porch as in the dining room.

Roomy wicker armchairs with red cushions and tack-upholstered backs provide a warm burst of color in the living area. Although vintage, they feel fresh and casual. The cushions and throws on the daybeds pick up on the happy color, as do other elements throughout the room. The vintage, dark green, blackout roller shades, once easy to find at the five-and-dime, are now difficult to replace.

The dining tables are good examples of the post–Depression era "make-do" approach perfected throughout the life of this cottage. Crafted by the owner's father, the finer of the two is a trestle table; its legs, fashioned from logs, add sturdiness and whimsy to the piece. The second table, which can be pushed against the first to accommodate more diners, is simply a picnic table left by the previous occupant.

The most valued characteristic of the table is that it can accommodate a crowd.

The dartboard takes the sting out of foggy and rainy days. Indeed, no cottage would be complete without shelves of board games, puzzles, and books collected by the occupants or left behind by guests. Reference books on local flora and fauna alternate with seafaring tales and a helter-skelter collection of novels.

In this bedroom, ample sunlight and the cool blue of the nautical bedspread creates the perfect setting for an afternoon nap. A pair of twin beds has been combined for king-size comfort. The simple, white curtains exemplify the "use-it-up" school of thought. When the owner inherited two dozen fine-cotton twin sheets from the 1930s, she made some into curtains and hung them on broom handles rather than rods.

The four-drawer painted dresser in the corner is familiar to those who have slept in cottage bedrooms. Green has long been a popular color for painted bedroom furniture, and here it enlivens the otherwise nearly unadorned room. A small painted chair and bedside table complete the bedroom tableau.

CHAPTER 2

island EDGE

Dramatically surrounded by tall pines and giant oaks, this cottage compound seems quiet, even lonely, when its residents are gone. Owned by six generations of the same family, this cottage has a deep and compelling history. Facing southeast, the site was originally an old farm pasture, and was later seized on as an excellent picnicking spot. One of the picnic pioneers, a woman who particularly delighted in the view, eventually became the matriarch of the house. She decided that such pleasurable dining should be a permanent affair and offered the local farmer a buyout of that wee bit of land for the family summer home. Since that auspicious day, the family has enjoyed cookouts and celebratory pig roasts on the same spot for more than a hundred years.

Like a Chanel suit, there is a sole bold flourish on the exterior of these dwellings: burgundy trim. The result is a setting that exudes proper grace and an unfussy, natural beauty that needs no adornment. The structures have more or less remained intact with no major changes over the years. New furniture pieces keep company with the cottage's original antiques; together, they make a clean, colorful space.

A great reverence for nature abides here. Tall trees harbor eagles and ospreys, while woods are home to deer, fox, raccoon, and skunk. An occasional moose finds its way from the woods into the clearing.

The cottage is reachable by a long dirt road that meanders through tall piney woods and passes a caretaker's cottage with its showy crimson dahlias. Along the road and into the woods, one feels a deep awareness of all the people who have enjoyed this land through the years.

The outbuildings all have exterior treatments that echo the main cottage itself, which underwent some interior reconfiguration in 1911. Before upgrades to the original plumbing in 1929 and the installation of electricity by generator (1924), then commercial power (1955), chores in the cottage and outbuildings were more laborious. But a good stiff wind and a clothesline work as well today as they did in 1878.

The land where the cottage now stands was a pasture when the original owner first camped here. In the early days of the house, the caretaking family planted a garden, from which they sold produce to the owner's family. Today, a garden of gorgeous red dahlias bursts into bloom in late summer and early autumn.

This spectacular stone fireplace door at left adds a real sense of place to this cottage. The rugged stones were hand-gathered in 1914 by the family matriarch's granddaughter. Her creative spirit is evident in the design, which she first laid out on the front lawn. She used so little mortar that the rocks seem to be held in place by gravity.

In this light-filled setting, vintage pieces mix jauntily with newer items. The Heywood Wakefield–style sofa, with its strong-lined arms, the rustic zigzag table, and the woven-backed armchair hold their own against colorful more contemporary pieces.

Two comfortable wicker chairs hold court by a window with fabulous views out to the porch and beyond, while whimsical teapots and a statuesque lamp impart modern color and form. The moss-colored cupboard in the corner controls the clutter and anchors the room, which is flooded with delicious sunlight.

Morning shadows thrown across the porch playfully intersect the curves and angles of the colorful furniture. The strong forms of the chairs and table echo the similar lines of the roof rafters and porch posts.

An antique rollback wicker armchair in the background and a wicker plant stand recall the Victorian era at the cottage, a time when boys and men wore coats and neckties and all meals were taken in the dining room. Gradually, though, the strict rules of Victorian etiquette softened: First, only breakfast was permitted on the porch, but eventually all meals could be taken outside.

Friends and family have enjoyed many hours of amusement playing games on this porch. A memoir lists darts, jar ring toss onto a lineup of twenty-eight cup hooks, turtle racing, with cardboard cutout turtles racing over a long cord tied to a chair, and skittles.

The second floor of the cottage gets flooded with sunshine, making the cheery yellow walls of this bedroom even more inviting. Unlike the walls throughout most of the cottage, the ones in this room are finished and painted. The distinctive shelving grids on the wall may have been a design solution—a creative use and decorative enhancement of the structural studs—and have been there as long as the owner's family can remember.

This green bedroom invites repose, with its fluffy pillows, vintage linens, and bedside tables with reading lamps. The board ceiling is painted a pale green, and when the sun is shining through the windows, being in the room feels as if you are in a soothing aquarium. The standout in this room is the chenille bedspread, with its array of blue-and-white eight-pointed stars.

CHAPTER 3

HILLTOP rustic

This cottage was created in the early 1900s when two structures from a nearby farm were moved to the site and joined together. The two simple red "boxes" no doubt provided a welcome rustic retreat for residents escaping from the ornately decorated wintertime houses of the period. Today, still stripped of the slightest embellishment, the cottage is a bare-feet-on-the-railing, song-singing hut that exudes freshness and the pure essence of cottage. Birds fly through the porch on their way to the berries, and the view down the hill never ends.

The porch features some classic cottage details. The wooden screen door, with its green paint and divided lower panel, has a rustic elegance sorely lacking in its modern-day aluminum counterparts. A distinctive bonus is the gentle "thwack!" it makes when it slams shut. For primitive souls, the porch stirs poetic wonder. A thousand stories have been told and remembered here—and a thousand more can be imagined just by walking past the porch.

The porch interior feels like a tree house, with unpainted rafters above it and leafy trees surrounding it. Classic folding woven-tape chairs, now collectible, are set around a yellow-painted table and make the porch an ideal gathering place. With age, the green chairs have taken on a humorous character, but they remain comfortable and strong. Their very survival throughout the years commands a loving respect. The rich purple, autumn-blooming asters were picked by the side of the road.

The strong green of the chairs and tables in the kitchen and dining room recall the spirit of the owner's grandmother, who loved to wield a paintbrush. The simple decor has been left mostly unchanged through the succession of three generations of the family that has spent summers here.

The simple overhead light, with its hemstitched shade and crocheted pull, has a sculptural presence as it hangs against the backdrop of the unfinished ceiling beams. Electricity wasn't available here until 1958. At first the owners resisted its charms, preferring the soft glow of kerosene lamps. When they finally signed on, they arranged for just one outlet for each room.

A cottage kitchen is the kind of place where wild blueberry pie and a cup of tea taste particularly good. The whitewashed walls and open shelving along with the gingham café curtains and vintage tablecloth add to the nostalgic feeling. The drop-arm counter off the sink offers welcome additional counter space.

The cottage seems put together like a puzzle. Its exposed wood boards, set both horizontally and vertically, along with many beams, studs, and door-ways, testify to the merging of two structures into one. The interior is given visual unity throughout by the unfinished wood, which has mellowed to a pleasing color.

The living room is a cozy place for family and friends to gather, especially on chilly days when the wood stove warms up the space. The old metal chair by the stove, purchased for very little from an old college friend, is a favorite reading spot.

CHAPTER 4
SHINGLE-STYLE cottage

Cottages today provide a sense of constancy that seems elusive in our often - chaotic lives. This cottage, a simpler expression of the huge shingle-style retreats built for wealthy families in the 1880s and 1890s, perches atop a grassy hill and overlooks a field that slopes down to a quiet, one-lane road. Between the field and the road, hundred-year-old rugosa rose hedges reach high above one's head. This cottage, this land, even these roses have been cared for by the family of the original owner since the house was completed in 1894. His great-great-grandchildren are the fifth generation to live here. From the porch's high-up roost, the family enjoys watching summer storms as they approach as well as expansive westerly views of magnificent sunsets.

The long period of time that this dwelling has been held by one family tells a beautiful story of the rich culture nourished and enjoyed in a cottage way of life. Because they are designed with fun, comfort, and ease foremost in mind, cottages are wonderfully compatible with familial lifestyle and very naturally handed down from one generation to the next.

Nestled in a field of rose bushes, with tall evergreens and a clear blue sky behind, the cottage cuts an elegant figure. With its arched entrance porch and attached gazebo, its strong, clean lines echo those of the simple 1807 yellow farmhouse located in the field below.

The head-to-toe use of shingles unifies the building and integrates it with the woods behind it. The cottage takes full advantage of its site with a wrap-around veranda that connects the indoor and outdoor living spaces.

Built for his young family by the architect Antoine Dorticos, a Cuban expatriate schooled in Paris, the cottage was preceded by another on its site. This first cottage, which was thought to have also functioned as a rooming house, perhaps to defray costs, was completed in 1885 but was destroyed by fire in 1894. Numerous commissions had refined Dorticos's talents, and the cottage he designed and built for his family displays his unique interpretation of the classic shingle style.

The gazebo-style porch offers a shaded enclosure for taking in the beauty of the view.

After walking though the enclosed space of the arched entrance porch, the open and airy first floor is a happy surprise. Windows and doors on all of the exterior walls flood sunlight into the area, and the open floor plan is deliberately uncluttered. French doors open out to extend the living room to the porch. Tall ceilings with open beams, all painted white, add to the bright spaciousness. The striking stone fireplace adds texture and brings nature into the room. The rocky local landscape is an integral part of the house, which sits upon twenty to thirty rock pilings as its foundation.

The window seats, original to the cottage, run along the perimeter of most of the first floor and allow for seating with a minimum of disruption to the floor plan. The cozy window seat next to the fireplace is deep and roomy enough to serve as an extra bed. Another long, angled window seat, with its handsome dark leather cushion (also original to the house), is nestled just below the window frames near the front entrance. The clever partitions at either end of the seat serve as privacy screens and subtle room delineators, and, together with the wide beadboard topped with a chair rail, create the illusion of a bench back.

A built-in hutch defines the dining-room space (opposite) with open shelves displaying colorful china. Painted white, the hutch is quietly ornamental, allowing the china to command the greater attention. The owner's great-uncle collected some of the pieces displayed in the hutch.

A bouquet of wildflowers in a glass pitcher is in delicate contrast to the round, dark, wood table, with its classical pedestal base. The sparse furnishing of the room brings into strong focus the spindly backs and curved aprons of the painted white chairs.

CHAPTER 5
COTTAGE AT
THE crossing

This cottage at the crossing of pathways reminds one of Hansel and Gretel–style thatched-roof dwellings. Although it appears rather small from the outside, there is a grand use of space inside. The L-shaped structure, with its multiplaned rooflines, is gracefully proportioned. The entrance hall is gracious, a room unto itself, and leads off to many adventurous hallways and doors. The second floor is rambling and open and has the feeling of a boarding house with its many bedrooms. The attic could hold a small bowling alley.

The cottage is a wondrous structure when one considers that no architects were involved in its construction, just local carpenters and tradesmen. The beautiful wood interior gives testament to the bounty of trees in the late 1800s and pause over the scarcity of treasured forests today. With its weathered shingles and informal plantings, including a spectacular climbing vine, this building could bear no other name than "cottage."

Flanked by a pair of white high-backed benches, the unassuming entry porch gives only a gentle hint of this cottage's considerable charms. Overflowing window boxes provide a dash of color against the facade's weathered tones.

One can take in the big-picture charm of a cottage
at first glance, but it is the small details that make
it sing. This corner of the sun porch door, with its
turquoise and brilliant blue trim, transcends expec-
tations.

With its expansive, arched French window and door, the latter trimmed in brilliant shades of turquoise and blue, the sun porch offers a protected space from which to enjoy the views. The interior shingled walls and downspout point to the space's previous life as an exterior porch. Sisal matting on the floor and a pair of wicker armchairs, one with a whimsical loop design, contribute to the comfortable feeling. A late-summer hydrangea flourishes in the window.

Bright green wicker lamps and a yellow bowl filled with pink impatiens offer counterpoints of color to the turquoise and blue window trim. The deep cushions of the wicker couch make it a most inviting spot, along with an old chest for putting up one's feet. Cheerful chintz fabric in a floral pattern and green metal vines snaking up either side of the arched window bring the idea of the garden inside. A simple wooden trestle table and caned chairs can be called into service for an indoor picnic luncheon.

Like the rest of the cottage, this gracious entry hall exhibits casual formality. The walls are clad in beadboard, but they remain rough with a subtle gray stain; this contrast sets the mood for the whole house. The warm grain of the wood is particularly evident on the frame of the double entry into the living room. The humble onion lantern, elevated to the status of a chandelier, casts a warm glow. The large hooked rugs—with an elegant star pattern that is both fancy and folksy—unify the room.

The pantry exhibits the more rustic side of the cottage's personality. Classic details such as the painted board walls, the peg-board display of pans, and the painted dresser add to the homey charm of this room. With a gentle breeze blowing the curtains out over a sunlit bowl of produce, the image is of a beautiful still life.

harborside

"I bought a moving painting." So says the owner of this 1905 cottage, regarding the panoramic view from his gracious porch of boats entering and leaving the harbor. How fitting that he should have first seen his future home from the deck of one of those boats during a day sail some years ago. The shingled cottages that seemed to hang onto the rocks so captured his fancy that he determined to live in one some day. The spirit of fun with which he has since embraced cottage living is infectious.

The symmetry of the cottage is simple and pure, as if a happy child had given his drawing to the builder. The house has three windows on top, with a door and windows directly below, wide, roomy front steps where lots of friends can sit, and a chimney right where it's supposed to be. The cottage, which the owner describes as "a box with a porch attached to it," seems a natural outgrowth of the site.

The interior reflects the tastes of one who is full of mischief and intellect. No one's wearing a tie here. Any decoration is as witty and unpretentious as the owner himself.

Jolly shades of aqua and yellow have been used in a casual way that makes the décor feel as if it just "happened." Inside and out, upstairs and down, these colors integrate an attitude of fun on every level. This is a quintessential playhouse for the grown-up kid who remembers that laughter is the ticket to living happily.

It seems that one could sit forever on the wrap-around porch, which is wide and inviting with wicker and rockers galore. The aqua highlights are bold and playful. The color, a mixture of ultramarine, grass green, and titanium, dances with other colors on the porch, including the red of an old rocker and the geraniums, the yellow of table and flowers.

The strong white shutters are as functional as they are lovely. Shutters provide essential protection against stormy off-season weather. The second-story roof projection made it perplexingly impossible to close the upstairs shutters, so they were taken down. Now, winter shutters are simply nailed on when summer is over. After an experiment with dark green trim, white was found to be better at standing up to the elements.

Although the vintage wicker chairs, rockers, and a blue-painted bench seem rooted to this porch, they had lives elsewhere before the owner, an avowed "junker," claimed them.

The porch is the great pride of this cottage, but there comes a time when one has to come inside. Luckily for those who do, the simple interior is conducive to socializing, dining, and sleeping.

The kitchen is basic and charming, enabling the host to entertain with ease. The colorful vintage shelf edging, utensils hung from nails on the wall, and an assortment of Pyrex came with the cottage and set the tone for a gentle renovation. New cabinets with cherry countertops and updated appliances were added to the mix.

The warm and lively dining room supports the owner's love of entertaining with aplomb. The unfinished open-frame construction, with especially high ceilings, gives the space an expansive feel. The warm patina of the board walls gains a jolt of excitement from the colorful painted chairs and buffet; the blue recalls the blue cushions on the porch, while the yellow and white are sunny and happy additions. "A cottage is supposed to be fun," the owner reasons. He knew the slightly over-the-top vintage chandelier would be perfect for the dining room.

A magnificent rocky landscape lies just outside, so the stone fireplace is right at home in the living room of the cottage. While it cuts a dashing figure, the fireplace also gives rise to a construction mystery: As the chimney climbs to the second floor, it twists for no apparent reason, making it nearly impossible to have it cleaned.

The Victorian patchwork crazy quilt belonged to the owner's grandmother. It suits the big wall with high ceilings and holds its own against the strong pattern of the stone fireplace. The room gets so much light that anything with a reflective surface, such as glass, cannot be used on the walls.

The upholstered pieces in the living room were chosen for their comfort: Pillows and throws make them irresistible. The cottage is meant to be low maintenance, and it has been decorated so not too much can go wrong.

A steeply pitched roofline creates angles that are challenging for tall guests, but the overall ceiling height makes the bedrooms seem more spacious than they are. The upholstered cotton-ticking head-boards and yellow spreads of the twin beds add to the charm of the unsophisticated room.

The bedrooms were kept spare and simple in keeping with cottage tradition. A shelf hung from the studs above the bed suggests a headboard. Vintage lacy shelf-edging, hung visibly with tacks, is a charming counterpoint to the modern-day baseball caps hung from a hook.

CHAPTER 7
WATERFRONT rambler

Originally an inn called the Albonegon, this waterfront structure was recently reborn as a private cottage. It rambles out over the water like an old covered bridge and sounds like one, too: As one walks from the front porch through the interior to the waterside porch, the old wood emits a symphony of creaks.

Crossing the threshold sends you back in time as you enter a vast yet intimate living room that feels like a steamboat stateroom. Gracious interiors are filled with soothing colors and textures from outside—woody browns, sage greens, rich and creamy whites, soft pinks, blues, rusts, and lavenders are reflections of stones, lichens, pine needles, water, seaweed, blueberries, and hydrangeas. The movement from exterior to interior is harmonious, seamless, and peaceful.

The cottage has the clean, spare quality of a country church, where hurrying ways are left at the door. But the old inn is rarely quiet these days, for it is now owned by one family of three generations—twenty-two people, twelve of them grandchildren under the age of fifteen. For some time the family searched for a cottage that could accommodate all of them. When the seventeen-room inn came on the market, a daughter joked that it was perfect—little did she know she was on to something. The family bought the late-1880s white clapboard structure and immediately set about transforming it into a comfortable, rambling, family-friendly cottage.

The transition required mostly a refreshing of the interiors, although the family made a determined effort not to change the essential feeling of the place. A fine line was drawn between what to keep as-is, such as the vintage sinks in each bedroom, and what to remove, such as wall-to-wall carpeting in the living room.

The changes were subtle and sympathetic enough so that in the first year, despite the presence of the "No Vacancy" sign in the front window, several unknowing longstanding patrons of the inn walked in looking for a room. One couple went so far as to let themselves into the kitchen for a cup of coffee.

The entry porch of the house welcomes visitors with a long bench, added by the owners and now peopled by families and friends—guests of the nonpaying kind who are presumably unconcerned by the "No Vacancy" sign.

This white-painted daybed was rescued from the old porch. With fresh new cushion covers and a compass-inspired needlepoint rug, the corner is a cozy spot for a temporary retreat. A rocking horse, dollhouse, and biscuit chest make it an area for the children to play.

The daybed has an unpainted, dark-wood mate in the living room. The two pieces have been identified as the most valuable furniture that came with the inn. Not everyone liked the daybeds at first, but they have become part of the family.

Although the painted sideboard and carved mirror evoke images of tea at the turn-of-the-century inn, these pieces were new additions to the dining room. Dappled sunlight, white paint, and reflections in the mirror create a dreamy setting. Painted glassware and china original to the inn connect those who enjoy the cottage today to guests of the past.

Some twenty bentwood chairs from the inn's dining room were refinished and recaned for family use. The dining room runs the length of the old porch, and the square tables can be put together in any number of configurations to suit the moment. For more than a hundred years, these tables have been ideal for playing bridge and board games, doing jigsaw puzzles, painting, writing letters, and dining.

One end of the living room is occupied by a handsome pool table purchased by the four sisters for their father after the family acquired the inn. Only grandchildren over age ten are allowed to use the pool table without adult supervision—a difficult rule to abide by if one is nine!

The heart of this family home beats strongly most notably in the living room, where the large fieldstone fireplace dominates this much-loved gathering spot. Everyone wants to be close to the rocks of the impressive fireplace, which were gathered from a nearby beach more than a century ago. The sign displays the inn's motto: "Determinedly Old-Fashioned."

Seating near the fire includes a wing chair, which retains its original upholstery, as well as a bench with flame-stitch needlepoint and a pair of painted green armchairs with woven backs and crewelwork cushions. The lamps in the living room are original to the inn. French doors on either side of the fireplace open into the dining room and extra living space. The simple construction of the cottage includes interior walls of painted matched boards—sometimes horizontal, sometimes vertical—and exposed-beam ceilings.

Open pantry shelving and a farm-house sink set the tone for the kitchen, famous for its muffins when the cottage was an inn. The kitchen was expanded after the family bought the property—they took down a wall between the innkeeper's living quarters and the kitchen—but it retains its vintage charm. The pantry shelving was extended to accommodate provisions, as well as china, pitchers, and casseroles from the inn days. New touches include beadboard walls, a vintage sink, cheerful yellow countertops, and the painted green floor.

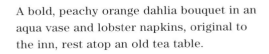

A bold, peachy orange dahlia bouquet in an aqua vase and lobster napkins, original to the inn, rest atop an old tea table.

CHAPTER 8

VICTORIAN treasure

A delightful museum ambience pervades the old paneled wood interior of this 1901 cottage, with its handsome and dramatic hearth. Six generations of one family have occupied it continuously for almost a century, first as renters and, since 1946, as owners. Victorian furniture, energized with lively fabrics, seems like an array of props on a summer-theater stage. Lazy green rockers and a canvas hammock are part of the collection of indoor and outdoor furniture that came with the cottage, adding to its deep sense of history.

From the porch one can rest in an old rocker and chat with neighbors on their missions to the post office or ice cream store. Constant activity down on the beach is like keeping a radio on low volume and ensures no one is ever lonely. Glorious sunsets are relished with family and friends.

Powerful arched brackets give dramatic architectural definition to the far end of the living room and provide structural supports for the stairway. This chunky formal woodwork, which repeats the southern pine of the horizontal board walls, contrasts with the informality of cottage life and the relaxing pleasures of the porch. Completely unpainted save for some dramatic dark green doors, the cottage interior is suffused with a uniform rich golden hue. The strong geometric pattern of the vintage living-room rug adds further visual interest to the space. The lampshades—also vintage, hand-pierced and hand-painted with voluptuous hydrangea-like blossoms—are flirty and bold.

Like many cottages, this one was sold to the current residents along with its furniture. As the original owner was a notable furniture manufacturer, some of the turn-of-the-century pieces probably came from his company. The fresh fabrics on recently reupholstered items give the dark-legged chairs a lighter look.

Bright sun hats hanging on one wall balance the blue-and-white china on the shelves of another. Below, the tableau of vintage lighting collected on the marble-topped console may seem quaint, but it proves useful when modern-day power occasionally fails.

This open china cupboard is cleverly constructed in a window alcove, making the most of an underutilized and sunny space.

If one spot defines the glory of this cottage and its porch, it is the hammock. Drifting along on this suspended canvas berth and looking out over the cove, a person can do some very serious daydreaming.

CHAPTER 9

WOODSY retreat

Rustic and graceful at the same time, this cottage is a fine place for a square dance, a fish fry, and hearty storytelling that results in boisterous laughter. Located deep in the woods, the cottage is nonetheless cheerful—its red, yellow, and green exterior give it a festive and merry quality.

The present owner's great-great-grandfather built this cottage in 1910 as a retreat for his family. They enjoyed the cottage for many years until it was sold out of the family in mid-century. As serendipity would have it, in the mid-1980s, the current owner had the joyous opportunity to reclaim his ancestral cottage.

The wrap-around porch has several areas that make it usable from spring through autumn: A glassed-in space for cool days, a screened-in area for bug season, and an open-air porch for perfect weather. The rocks surrounding the house are also its support; an expanse of ledge beneath the cottage is the main foundation.

The original house was most likely rectangular, with the wrap-around porch continuing all along the side. When the time came to add an indoor bathroom, the new side section was added and the porch abbreviated. The second level of the addition contains a small bedroom.

The humble interior, little changed from when it was first built, offers a space that's intimate and cozy—perfect for settling into restful conversation. The inside of some door casings still show the family's penciled-in growth charts, which date back to the early 1900s—a sweet reminder of loved ones and their history in the cottage.

The yellow and green trim feels fresh and modern, yet the color combination has been in place for almost a century. The exuberant use of yellow paint for the porch ceilings and railings unifies the space with the rest of the exterior, and lends a cheerful quality to the space in even the worst weather.

The sunny yellow on the walls of the kitchen is a showstopper. The geometric pattern of the vintage linoleum floors adds pizzazz without fuss.

The white walls and ceiling of the glassed-in porch seem almost chaste compared with the vivid color scheme of the open porch. This enclosed section is a comfortable space in all seasons. The window valance brings some red and yellow into the room without obscuring the views. The cottage was purchased (with contents) so the current owners started off with a room full of vintage wicker and rocking chairs.

While all of the exposed frame walls on the first floor are painted, the bedrooms upstairs remain unfinished. With its white painted dresser, bed, and chair, and simple white curtains and bedspread, this inviting room offers peace and quiet. Just a hint of the exterior trim colors shows in the window.

A pair of green Adirondack chairs offers an off-porch resting place.

The late-summer season for wild blueberries is short but sweet. A few bushes on the property yield a handful for cereal, while the boxes upon boxes at local markets and roadside stands sell out early in the day.

PART III
Fresh Ideas

One wonderful aspect of owning a cottage today is that it gives us license to do something adventurous and fun with its decoration. Most of us hesitate to be bold with the design and furnishing of our day-to-day dwellings, but cottagers are blessed with the freedom to be untamed, even foolish, to create spaces that are as romantic and imaginative as we dare them to be.

This section features a selection of cottages that have taken the best elements of the past and distilled them into a charismatic and refreshingly simple style that truly reflects each owner's unpretentious and energetic way of living. Colors are tested and tasted with the eyes—like imaginative ingredients in a recipe for a feast that comforts and inspires. Bold blue porch chairs that reflect the shades of water, a papaya-hued dining room that arouses conversation, a bright, sunlit bedroom, shingle siding stained the shade of lacy hemlocks, and sky-blue painted floors—all of these details blend into and brighten environments.

The spaces inside these homes resonate with a cottage feeling of simple living that's enjoyed every day. Snug and cushy sofas with bright linen slipcovers and vintage cloth pillows sit next to the fireplace. Charming antique quilts invite families to read and rest together in tender comfort. Antique wicker and painted flea market tables combined with newer, casual pieces and contemporary artwork results in "accidental decorating." Pantries and open shelving are as fashionable as they are functional, providing easy access and encouraging entertaining.

Collections of shells and rocks are evidence of nature's importance, just as compositions of antique dishes, pottery, and textiles pay homage to the history of the cottage and create an immediate sense of connection to family and days gone by. Outside, old doors and windows, well-worn pathways, a weathered trellis, and tall trees that have stood on the property long before the cottage was built are equally evocative.

Today's cottages continue to celebrate the beauty of nature through gardens that have thrived for more than a hundred years and cheerful window boxes filled with bright flowers that welcome family and friends. Likewise, the porch still holds strong as the focal point for friends and family to relax, read, dine, take in the view—and simply enjoy each other's company in a setting that has captured the romance of summer for generations.

rockledge

This cottage, christened Rockledge, is a fresh interpretation of a classic melody. The owners' fun-loving taste is everywhere. Bright color on floors and walls creates a jazzy space where collections of contemporary artwork and crafts mix wonderfully with the treasures from the cottage's past. Used only as a summer retreat in Victorian times, the little house is now enjoyed all year round.

A little more than a century after it was built, this 1885 Second Empire–style structure with its characteristic mansard roof was given a loving, restorative face lift. Additions had diminished its profile (a second-story room extended over the driveway on stilts), and the building had been clad in green aluminum siding. Yet the cottage had much to recommend it. The new owners knew clearly what they wanted.

They protected and reused century-old materials such as doors, knobs, and original wood floors. If they closed one doorway, they widened another. They refurbished the plaster walls with horsehair lathing. The renovation took five years and was done in stages, but the old gal was brought back to life.

The elegant lines of the mansard roof were enhanced by the pergola at the back of the cottage. The bracketed cornices, which appear in a striking regular pattern around the cottage's exterior, are cleverly repeated in the pergola's crossbeams. All of the woodwork wears a unifying crisp coat of white paint.

The pergola and the stone wall, topped by a wood fence, were added to the cottage just recently, after the restoration had had a chance to settle. Both provide a sense of privacy to the backyard, and many people say they look as if they have been there forever—the ultimate compliment. The owners adore gardening, and the wall provides a striking backdrop for their plantings. A large perennial garden that had been planted in the front of the property was shifted to new beds inside the stone wall, yielding a new garden that appeared fairly mature in short order. Today, a desire to make a happy, casual place for guests and neighborhood children is evident everywhere, and several windows offer unexpected and intimate views. A "sunset" room is an effusive and festive statement of the simple joys of life, enjoyed year-round.

This screened-in porch was originally a glassed-in sunroom. Doors on either end allow access to the front and back of the porch. The screened area effectively becomes a playroom for the owners' Maine coon cat, which is not allowed outside. She sits on the bench and natters at birds, bugs, and visiting cats on the other side of the screen.

Small-scale furniture makes the most of the long narrow room. A bistro table and chair in vibrant orange, found at a favorite local shop, provide a fetching spot for a quiet lunch.

The dining-room furniture, including the painted hutch (opposite), was purchased with the cottage. The hutch is filled with china used by all three of the families that have occupied the house. On the top shelf, English teacups from the owner's paternal grandmother mix with white-and-gold wedding china from the cottage's first matriarch.

The sunny apricot of the dining-room walls (above) replaced some rather unattractive 1950s wall-paper that the owners stripped off. Stunned by all of the wallpaper in the cottage—in some rooms there was different wallpaper on the ceiling and the walls—they lived with stripped white walls for the first year, then inched their way into the color one sees now.

After they tried and rejected a bolder palette, they had the area above the crown molding repainted in the same soft apricot of the walls. The decorative painter who created this frieze of leaves and flowers also hand-painted the striped walls in the entry hall.

This casual living room was a more formal parlor in the early decades of the cottage. Photographs from 1886 show a mix of oriental rugs, heavy brocade fabrics, dark-wood furniture, and wonderfully airy rattan chairs; images from 1914 show a change to elaborately festooned wallpaper. By the time the current owners came to the cottage, the mauve-painted woodwork and wallpaper made the room dreary and dark.

The old green paint on the porch door was one inspiration for the new color scheme; the French blue on part of the floor was another. The chairs and small couches were slipcovered, and the denim sofa, widely known among guests for its nap-inducing qualities, was purchased with comfort in mind.

Two bedrooms off the sunset room have a connecting door, perfect for guests with small children. The cottage came with a collection of vintage cast-iron doorstops, which are useful for keeping doors from blowing shut in a cross-breeze. A vintage painted spool bed and bamboo standing shelf also came with the cottage.

The lovely glow of the setting sun, spectacular from this second-story room, inspired the color for the walls, which were almost overwhelming until the furniture, rug, and paintings were brought in. The chunky plum bench, multicolored striped rug, and dark rattan chairs bring balance to the room.

Stars pop up everywhere, often in subtle or unexpected places: On a twig stool, a crocheted throw, a chenille pillow. At one end of the living room, a vintage window box adorned with wood stars sits on top of an old painted chest found in a bedroom of the cottage. Old stars from building facades appear above doorways and windows.

The cottage's old kitchen was far short of charming. Part of a slap-dash addition to the original building, which was rock-solid, the kitchen and upstairs rooms were torn down, then built back. This resulted in losing a back staircase but gaining a kitchen pantry, a laundry, and a full bath.

The pantry, with its sunny window, is a great place to mix and measure for baking. On one side, open shelves hold stacks of bowls, plates, and accessories for casual dining; on the other, foodstuffs.

Window dormers create a strong line in the room, but the substantial bed, made of reclaimed architectural elements from the porch, has the presence to stand next to them.

When the new owners took possession of the cottage, they found the bedrooms charmingly furnished with painted dressers. A favorite tall model has lots of fancy trim.

CHAPTER 11

GARDENSIDE cottage

Originally this marvelous cottage from the Victorian era had cedar shingles and working shutters. Transformed twenty years ago from a rental house to a treasured summer cottage for an expanding family, this dreamy Victorian clapboard offers a good example of how cottagers of our day live. The current owners started life at the cottage with four young children and are now pleased that a third generation will soon enjoy it, too. The room over the furnace, which their children appropriated in the early days and christened the "clubhouse," is ready and waiting for a grandchild.

This rambling and pristine family getaway is furnished with pieces that were inherited, came with the cottage, and purchased locally as accents—all of which reflect both the current owners' taste and the ongoing traditions of cottage life. The classic lines of the cottage are modified by the addition of dormers, bay windows, and corner balconies on the second and third floors. These architectural nooks and crannies give character to the seven upstairs guest bedrooms.

Built in the 1890s, the cottage, known as Gardenside, was once one of a collection of rental units originally associated with a four-story Queen Anne–style inn. The houses each bear the design of the different contractors hired to build them. The cottages were often rented year after year by the same families, who treated them as summer homes. While the cottages had fully equipped kitchens, meals could be taken at or delivered by the inn, and all social functions, such as tea dances, could be attended by the cottage renters. After the entire property—inn and cottages—was sold in 1963, the inn was razed and the cottages were sold off individually.

A unifying coat of crisp white paint keeps the many fanciful elements of the porch architecture in check. A visual delight, the carpentry details include chamfered posts topped with solid curvy brackets, rafters ending with pronounced ball shapes, and a wavy "picket" at the roof slope. The railing sports a dignified geometric pattern that echoes some of the window mullions.

Mature copper beech, apple, and maple trees form a verdant backdrop for the white cottage, while border gardens and the hot pink petunias spilling out of hanging baskets offer painterly splashes of color.

The 1930s suite of rattan porch furniture received a coat of white paint and blue cushions when it was brought from the Connecticut home of one of the owner's parents. The inviting deep curve of the Pawleys Island hammock brings a touch of the South Carolina coast to the summer cottage.

The living room is an elegant oasis. The cool white walls and couch are offset by the colors of the rug, curtains, and patchwork quilt. The white-painted fireplace—a quiet masterpiece—has carved and turned embellishments that are both playful and refined.

Soft light from the window brightens the vintage wisteria wallpaper in the narrow stairwell, echoing the fact that at one time, a mature wisteria climbed up the exterior of the cottage. The landing derives its quiet elegance from nineteenth-century details such as the newel post and the pattern of the mullioned windows. An old-fashioned bouquet of pink phlox, burgundy zinnias, and Queen Anne's lace from the cottage's August garden is set on the deep windowsill.

The butler's pantry remains as it was when the cottage was purchased, including its vintage gold linoleum. The kitchen was well equipped when it was built as a rental cottage, but has not been much improved over the decades. The thick cherry countertop and blue-painted cabinets with carved drawer handles are conveniently located next to the dining room.

This cottage bathroom is remarkable for its purity and simplicity. The curvy claw-foot tub plays coquette to the dignified lines of the room's southern pine floorboards, wainscoting, and paneled door. As in many cottages, the soap holder hangs onto the curved tub edge.

A bouquet of sweet peas ornaments this old-fashioned bedroom, which is furnished to perfection with twin beds and vintage pink appliqué quilts, a caned rocking chair, and a classic white-painted dresser topped with a framed mirror. The dresser and rocker came with the cottage. Sunlight makes the white Priscilla curtains and the southern pine floors glow.

The impressive carved-mahogany
headboard in this bedroom has met
its match in the vivid patchwork
quilt from a local shop. Ample light
from the bay window gives the room
a sunny disposition.

CHAPTER 12
farmhouse COTTAGE

This farmhouse cottage is a beautiful example of Shaker spareness mixed with today's comfort and color. The owners, who are writers and worldwide travelers, have created a peaceful retreat for immersing themselves in the renewing solitude of the natural world.

Thorough scouring, painting, and de-cluttering have helped create a timeless dwelling far from interstate highways and airports. The deck provides a natural flow from farmhouse to field, offering views of the landscape, fields, water, and, in season, flocks of migrating geese. The tranquility of the setting is pervasive.

This cottage started life as two shed buildings on the farm property, and the original farmhouse still stands nearby. When the owners purchased the property, the structures were in great disrepair. Knowing that part of the kitchen, the oldest area of the house, dated from the early 1800s, they embarked on a project to restore as much of the original building as possible and to introduce modern conveniences subtly.

As with many farmhouses, this home's history included the gradual addition and connection of outbuildings to the main house, as well as visible alterations dating from different eras. An old photograph helped the owners and their restoration-minded local contractor return to the structure details that had been missing for years—among them the wrap-around porch, which is now screened-in and has a hot tub cleverly nestled into a corner to take advantage of the afternoon sun. Thirty-six double-hung two-over-two windows were also put in to replicate windows from the period when the house was built.

The visitor who wanders through the rooms of this renovated cottage feels physical joy simply from being in this delightful space. Uncluttered and restful spaces give movement free rein. Sun streams through the big windows, reflecting off the honey-colored wood floors and painted walls in a continual dance of light. There is also a marvelous, hard-to-define interior stirring caused by surprising jolts of color in unexpected places and a merging of the house's original primitive spirit with a modern-day sensibility. The two owners have created a place for rest, peaceful work, and daydreaming.

Having honored various changes to the structure over the course of two centuries, they are now building a Victorian-style, one-room meadow house/writer's studio on the property. The fourteen-by-sixteen-foot building, with a porch, will not follow the historical trend and be physically connected to the main house, but it will be one with it in spirit.

At the back of the house, a wonderful "porch" projects from above the doorway, probably added to the facade in the Civil War era. As an ornamental detail, the canopy projection and its deep, carved support brackets give a little punch to the otherwise almost austere exterior; practically, it provides shelter from rain and sun.

By the time the owners bought the farmhouse in 1990, no part of its original wrap-around porch remained. An old photograph gave them an idea of what it had looked like and inspired them to rebuild it. The architectural details of the new porch give the farmhouse a crisp cottage feel. In the corner, a white post and corbel frame the edge of the period pale blue porch ceiling, which makes the sky seem a part of the house.

The aqua walls of a guest bedroom glow on a sunny day. The wide pine floors and antique quilts recall the textures and tones of earlier centuries.

The bedrooms have visual continuity due to the distinctive colors, vintage quilts, and cottage furniture that they share, but they are sunny individualists nonetheless. Yellow walls in the room below make it feel happy no matter how temperamental the weather.

Guests are charmed by the yellow bathroom's old-fashioned sink, with its separate hot and cold faucets and drain plug on a chain, as well as the deep, old claw-foot tub. This was the only full bath in the house when the owners bought it, although they have since made a second bath out of a bedroom. They kept the original claw-foot tub and wall-mounted sink, but decided to replace the linoleum on the floor with black-bordered white tiles. The wainscoting is original to the room.

The kitchen was a labor of love for both the owners and the carpenter who helped them reclaim it. A few pieces of the beadboard wall and ceiling are original to the oldest part of the house; new beadboard was matched as closely to it as possible. The room was basically taken apart and rebuilt on site, with new cabinets designed to look as if they had always been there.

The kitchen's old wood stove was converted to kerosene stove, and the nickel hardware was sent away to be re-dipped. An old slate sink, an extra refrigerator, and the laundry are tucked away in a connecting room between the kitchen and barn, freeing up space in the main kitchen.

The owners kept the dining room spare, letting the integrity of the space guide them in its furnishing. Papaya-pumpkin hued walls and crisp white beadboard make a lovely setting for the old table and chairs. The top of the farm table was made from old English pine boards, then placed upon sturdy legs. The mellow wood tones complement the cottage floors, once concealed beneath multiple layers of mismatched linoleum.

The lines of the Appalachian-style rocking chair and dining room chair in the distance are artful in the stillness of the afternoon. The wonderful glow from the dining room's yellow walls, augmented by streaming sunshine, provide a bright yet soothing corner for reading and reflection.

CHAPTER 13
SEA captain's RESCUE

This charming little village home was originally built as a sea captain's summer cottage in the 1890s. Even though it has had four different owners over the last century, nothing had been changed to mar its graceful personality. But when its current owners, a young couple, discovered it around 1990, it was in a much neglected state.

The new owners put their enthusiasm and energy into a glorious rebirth for the structure, refitting it from the ground up over one long winter. While the cottage was raised and a cellar put in, the owners remained in the house. The little heat they enjoyed was from the dependable old fireplace, built by the sea captain himself.

The following summer, the ornamental shingles on the upper part of the cottage were taken down, sanded, painted anew, and refitted. One porch was removed and another added, and the back of the house was extended by ten feet. The front door and the garden gates and paths were widened so that two people can now pass through at the same time. The elegant little lady now shines again.

This favorite meeting spot for locals a hundred years ago remains a center of activity today. One of the owners, a landscape designer, has created a cottage garden and year-round retreat where she brings her clients to survey the blooms of hundreds of varieties of flowers.

The painted bench and rockers, found in the cottage, are dressed up for the summer season with pillows covered in striped bark cloth. Hanging flower baskets attract many hummingbirds. Large candle vases are lit on summer evenings.

The backyard is a lush sanctuary, which evolved according to a seven-year, garden-design plan. The extension off the back of the cottage made room for a master bedroom upstairs that opens out to an inviting deck and morning sun. On the ground floor, the extra space allowed for a roomier kitchen and a cozy south-facing parlor from which the gardens can be readily enjoyed.

These Adirondack chairs are painted a stylish color, a combination one of the owners mixed from shades of periwinkle and marine blue. The old wooden plant stand was a birthday gift to coordinate with the painted bench found in the cottage.

An old outhouse at the end of the
driveway was transformed into the
garden shed (right). To enter the
backyard gardens, one passes quite
magically through an arbor of climbing hydrangeas. A smaller version of
the garden shed was built to store
wood for the fireplace (below).
Butterfly plants and potted flowers
grow with abandon and surround
the sheds and stone terrace.

Various shades of blue and green fill
a paneled back passageway leading
to the blues and greens of the great
outdoors. A lively composition of
traditional cottage textures and colors, the narrow space comes alive
with the interesting fishing motif on
the floor and family photographs on
the wall.

An old blue-painted cupboard
anchors the space and keeps a
library of gardening books at the
ready. The classic old painted chair
was found in the attic.

An antique black slate sink adds a dramatic sculptural quality to a space dominated by the colors of summer—blue, green, and white—and the natural lacework of scented geraniums and ferns. A local antique store yielded the fish above the sink, a perfect decorative touch for this former sea captain's abode.

The warm, honey-colored wood of this old blanket chest shows up strikingly against the creamy paneling on the wall. The chest houses the owner's antique glass holiday decorations. Antique molding, made into a frame for an old beveled mirror, gives the effect of another window and bounces additional light into the room.

The cupboard, originally a built-in from an old Quebec farmhouse, now highlights a collection of yellowware and ironstone.

The southeastern corner of the cottage is the favored sitting spot. In warm weather there is always a fragrant wind blowing through the open windows. An old Chippendale-style sofa, one of the owner's mother's, has a green summer-ticking slipcover. Sofas with one long cushion are the owners' favorites; additional throw pillows offering functional comfort. The flowers on the pillow fabrics are the same as those blooming outside in the garden—roses, hydrangeas, and lilacs.

A little table from a Quebec flea market serves as a perfect cocktail table. The new blue wooden chairs are from a local garden shop, selected "because big, comfy informal chairs that make you think of the ocean are perfect in this spot," said one owner. At the window, morning sun streams through wisteria vines. Scallop shells found on a local beach and sea glass collected in jars are reminders of delightfully aimless summer days.

This corner of the living room was once part of the front screened-in porch, which ended at the edge of the blue carpet. Now it's a cozy spot for reading and playing board games. The tailored look of the upholstery keeps fussiness at bay. A glorious mixture of old and new pieces spice up this space.

Pine paneling, painted creamy white, enhances the look of a tiny guest room. The antique bed was found in Quebec province, the petite, painted side table at a local flea market. Watercolor scenes by village residents add local flair. Daylight filters through curtains made from new French bed linens. At night the beaded shades of the candle lamps lend an aura of romance.

Morning sun pours through the French doors and
sixteen-paned upper window of this master bedroom. The English pine bed is surrounded by
antique pieces from the grandmother of one of the
owners. The cardinal prints—lovingly renovated,
then replaced in the original frames—sing to each
other across the room and are cherished for their
graceful connection to the past.

CHAPTER 14
A **brand-new** COTTAGE

This brand-new cottage-bungalow is nestled in the woods among several early 1900s cottages that provided its inspiration. The structure follows the contours of the land, and surrounding tall pines provide a peaceful setting. A score of blueberry bushes planted by the front entrance provide luscious picking in August and bold red color in autumn.

The house setting itself is intimate among the trees yet open to the neighborhood and all its happenings. The lot is wide to the road, allowing the owners to see and enjoy many gardens and neighbors. Important activities can be observed from the kitchen windows—kids running for the bus, a neighbor training for a marathon, dogs visiting each other and prowling about.

The owners are artists and designers who enjoy color and play with it throughout this lively space, using bold, translucent shades to reflect the sunlight's energy. A workshop-studio lets the couple incorporate their woodworking and painting pleasures into their everyday living.

The designer-owners of this house are smitten with the playful possibilities of structure. Given the opportunity to build a turn-of-the-new-century cottage, this pair drew upon their knowledge of cottage vernacular as well as their own well-defined artistic sensibilities. The result is a dwelling that is perfectly located on its site and uses materials that reflect the setting—the cedar shingle siding, for instance, suits the wooded environment. Informed by its owners' highly personal vision, the home transforms the cottage vernacular while celebrating it.

This cottage is a series of three connecting huts, each opening to the other, and sits protected deep in a wooded lot. The joined structures—a shop-studio, a dining hall, and living area—cascade down the hill and create a pavilion effect among old hemlocks and pines. The small workshop-studio is a shared by the owners, who also make furniture.

In the living area, two stone steps lead one down into the dining hall, which in turn opens up into the great room of the living area. Here, the concept of "connecting" is celebrated. When one is reading at the far end of the living space, there is recognition of activity down in the workshop, even when the windowed doors are closed.

The tropical blue background of the Art Deco-style printed slipcovers contrasts in a lively way with the coral walls and ochre couches. The ocean blue mimics the shade in various paintings of water and fish, and also the vintage pottery pieces.

A witty play on the traditional cottage stone fireplace, this one leaves the stones—and the mantel—out of the equation. Using modern materials, the fireplace and chimney are given a dramatic overcoat of charcoal-pigmented cement. Three chairs gather around the hearth, one of many small "rooms" created by furniture groupings within the open floor plan.

When neighbors come over for dinner, this game corner (opposite) is where all the kids settle. With large windows that face southwest into the deep woods, it's a lovely spot in the late afternoon. An outdoor sauna, which the owners just completed, sits near the edge of the woods and brings immense pleasure on cold evenings.

A curvy pair of couches in bold ocher linen forms their own social club in the living room. Red birch flooring and the sunset-colored walls, achieved by applying washes of coral, peach, and red, create a warm atmosphere and echo some of the traditional cottage colors. Double windows in the far corner open the room up to a living landscape that changes with the seasons.

The home office tucked into a corner is a joyous confluence of wood: Thick, horizontal hemlock beams; a lush expanse of red birch floors; a cherry plank bench; a curly maple writing desk; a rustic, dark wood bench table; and the windows filled with views of trees.

The double windows, hung almost floor to ceiling throughout the first floor, flood the space with light and celebrate wood by allowing the mature trees on the property to be enjoyed from inside. The cottage seems to understand its place in this sylvan setting.

The writing desk was crafted by the owner, as was the low bench made from a piece of cherry wood placed atop two curly-maple sawhorses. Files and catalogs can lay flat atop the plank or in baskets below. An oriental rug with woodsy colors gives texture and definition to the space.

This sleek and artful kitchen has surprising precedents in vernacular cottage kitchens. The paneled walls, cast-iron sink, sturdy open shelving with bracket supports, and hanging lights are found in many an early cottage. Likewise, the vintage American pottery bowls, collected for their color, form, and function, are seen time and again in old cottage kitchens. The double-basin cast-iron sink, found intact in its 1948 crate, is classic cottage style.

The polished cement counters, poured by the owners, stainless steel dishwasher, and deep purple-painted cabinets are hallmarks of a twenty-first-century kitchen—a cottage state of mind in a modern, year-round setting.

The dining space was inspired by a summer camp in North Carolina, where the dining hall was long with many windows, and deep in the woods. Here, ocher walls bring the space into the new century. At night, strung across the ceiling like Chinese lanterns, handmade paper lights illuminate the space. A pair of curly-maple planks forms the linear dining table.

The wall of floor-to-ceiling windows along with the scored cement floor suggest the feeling of a porch, making wicker and rattan furniture appropriate to the space. Antique rattan chairs sport fantastic kilim cushions, giving them the oriental feeling so coveted by Victorians. The clean lines of the chairs are matched by those of the wicker table and the elegant antique wicker chaise.

At the far end of the cottage is the workshop. Here, a wall of windows from a public library, found at an architectural salvage house, separates the workspace from the living space. A glass door on a barn-door slider enables the owners to remain connected to the rest of the house when working in the enclosed space.

This tub was discovered abandoned in a pasture, brought home, and refinished to a sparkling state.

The guest bedroom is welcoming
with a spring green beadboard
daybed and vintage chenille
coverlet. A painted wicker night-
stand with a reading lamp and
a comfortable reading chair with
bright cushions complete the
restful composition.

A rustic window shutter above the
bed in this room can be opened
to let in westerly summer breezes.
The bedroom door is one of six
matching ones found in an architectural salvage house and used
throughout the second floor. The
old wall shelf retains its vivid shade
of blue. Support brackets are a
wonderful cottage detail that is
used inside and outside this house.

Binoculars rest at the window
for the arrival of woodpeckers,
cardinals, chickadees, and cedar
waxwings.

Sources

furnishings:

Lee Industries
PO Box 26
Newton, North Carolina 28658
828 464 8318

Maine Cottage
PO Box 935
Yarmouth, Maine 04096
207 846 1430

lighting:

Altamira Lighting
79 Joyce Street
Warren, Rhode Island 02885
401 245 7676

Galbraith & Paul
307 North Third Street
Philadelphia, Pennsylvania 19106
215 923 4632

textiles:

Full Swing Textiles
474 Thames Street
Newport, Rhode Island 02840
401 849 9494
Barkcloth deco designs

Cuddledown
231 Route One
Freeport, Maine 04032
207 865 1713
Coverlets and pillows

Sara Hotchkiss Rugs
28 Pitcher Road
Waldoboro, Maine 04572
207 832 8133

paintings:

Greenhut Galleries
140 Middle Street
Portland, Maine 04101
207 772 2693

Goldsmith Gallery
41 Commercial Street
Boothbay Harbor, Maine 04538
207 633 6252

Photo Credits

Acknowledgments

The author wishes to give special thanks to: my editor, Constance Herndon, assistant editor, Trudi Bartow, and designer, Nina Barnett for patiently nurturing this idea into reality; Margaret Chase for making the connection; Patricia O'Shaughnessy for her spirited vision; Mildred Kinney, Mike Darling, Gail Cinelli, Elizabeth Burns, Marty Trower, Robert Pile, Alice Carter, Jane Campbell, Sandi Stackhouse, Stephanie Pilk, Lauren Ostis, and Deb Merrill, all true friends and cottage enthusiasts; and Estabrook Greenhouses, the Chebeague Island, Southport Island, and Yarmouth Historical Societies, Greater Portland Landmarks, Casco Bay Ferry Service, Chebeague Island Taxi, and all who welcomed us into their homes and shared their histories and love of cottages. To Leisa Crane for her sprightly additions to the text and captions, and for many hours of devoted research. And to Dennis Welsh for his remarkable images and continual friendship.

Index

Published in 2008 by Stewart, Tabori & Chang
An imprint of Harry N. Abrams, Inc.

Originally published in hardcover in 2003 by Stewart, Tabori & Chang

Library Of Congress Cataloging-in-Publication Data
Bass, Carol
       The Cottage Book: living simple and easy/ Carol Bass;
Photographs by Dennis Welsh
       p. cm.
Includes index
ISBN: 978-1-58479-678-7
1. Cottages—Decoration—United States.
I. Welsh, Dennis. II. Title.

NK2195.C67 B37 2003
747'.8837—dc21

2002191135

Design by Nina Barnett
Cover design by Alissa Faden

The text of this book was composed in ITC Century.

Printed in China
10 9 8 7 6 5 4 3 2

harry n. abrams, inc.
a subsidiary of La Martinière Groupe
115 West 18th Street
New York, NY 10011
www.hnabooks.com

Dedication

For Ruby, for Bob, and for my joyous children,
Hannah, Molly, Sam, and Ryan.